Let's Find Out About the Hospital

Let's Find Out About the Hospital

by Eleanor Kay, R.N.

illustrated by William Brooks

FRANKLIN WATTS | NEW YORK | LONDON

SBN 531-00072-9
Copyright © 1971 by Franklin Watts, Inc.
Library of Congress Catalog Card Number: 75-131145
Printed in the United States of America

Have you ever seen an ambulance go whizzing down the street?

Its red light flashes.

The siren whines.

Cars and trucks pull over to the side of the road to let the ambulance pass.

Drivers in the cars and trucks know that the ambulance is taking someone to the hospital.

The ambulance must get to the hospital quickly.

People don't always go to the hospital in
 an ambulance.
But they do go to the hospital because they
 are sick.
Or because they have been hurt in an
 accident.
Or because a baby is going to be born.

There are lots of reasons to go to the
 hospital.
But the best reason is to get well quickly
 and go home again.

There are many things to see in a hospital.
Many different kinds of people work there.
You may be very sick when you go to the
    hospital.
But everything will be done to make you
    well again soon.

If you go to the hospital, you will be called by a new name.

You will be called a *patient*.

A patient may be big or little, young or old.

Patients go to the hospital to be taken care of by the people who work there.

A patient is very special in a hospital.

It is good to know that you are special when you are a patient.

Doctors think that patients are special.
In a hospital, doctors usually wear white suits.
Their shoes make whispering sounds when they walk by.
Doctors examine patients to see what is wrong with them.
They want to help patients get well quickly.

There are many kinds of doctors in a hospital.
Some doctors are called *interns*.
Other doctors are called *residents*.
Doctors who work in the operating room are called *surgeons*.

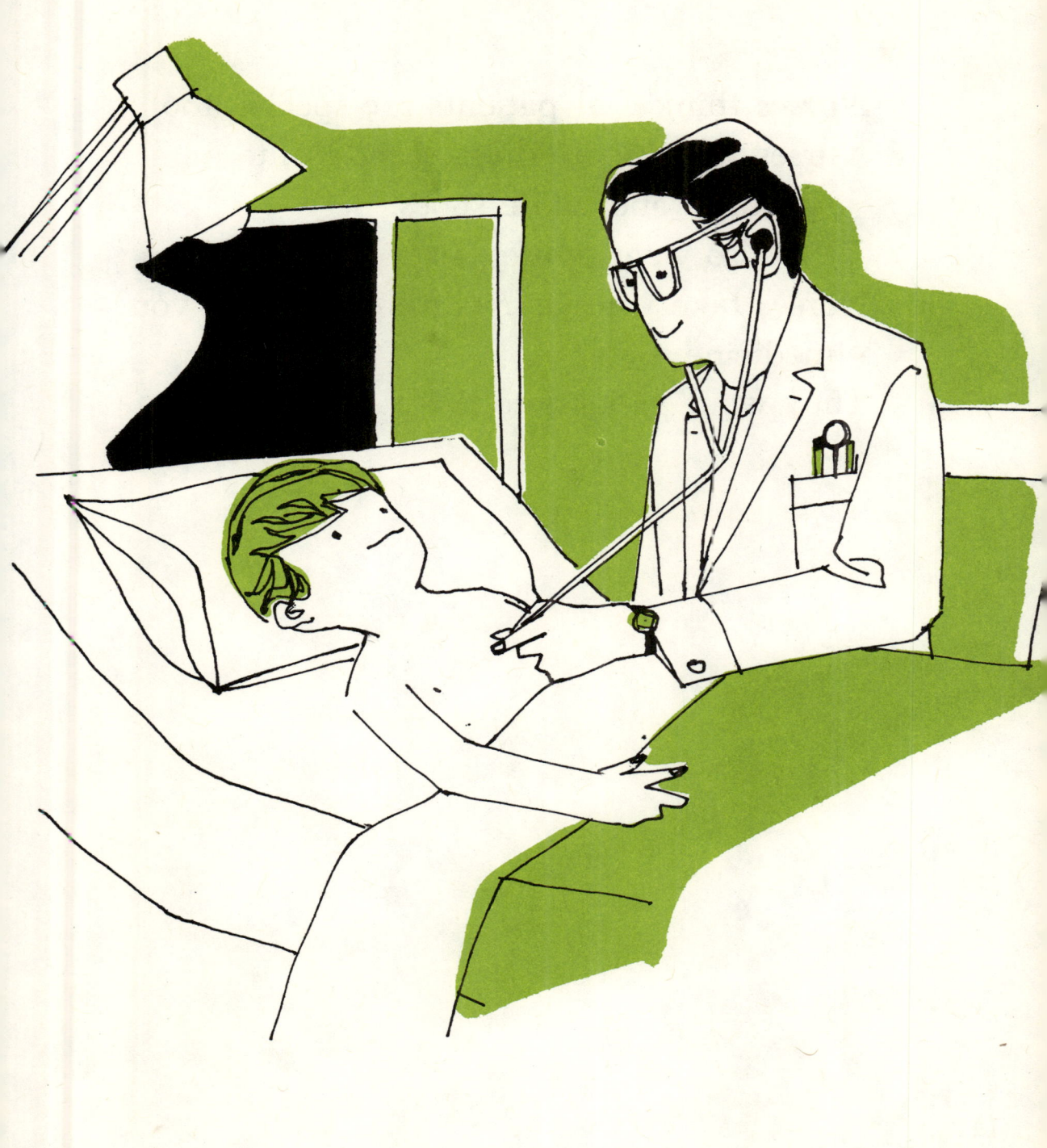

Nurses think that patients are special, too.
Nurses wear white dresses and white stockings and white shoes.
They also wear white caps.
Nurses take your temperature and give you medicine.
They want patients to get well soon, too.

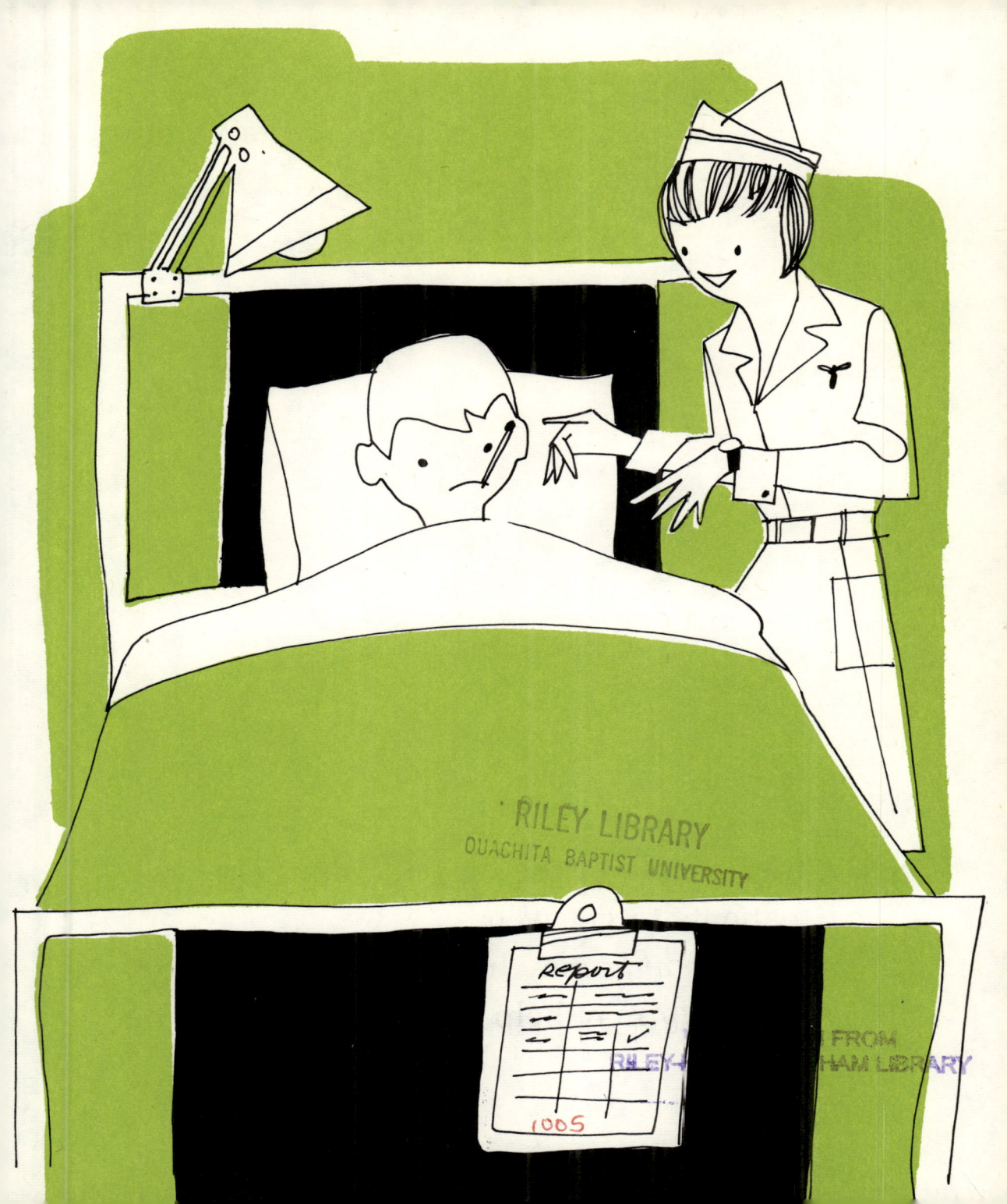

Other people in the hospital also help
   patients to get well.
A *nurse's aide* may help you get into bed.
An *orderly* may help you to walk down the
   hall.

A hospital patient sometimes stays in a room by himself.
Or with one or two other people.
A very large hospital room with lots of patients in it is called a *ward*.

Hospital rooms are bright and clean.
Everything in the hospital is kept as clean as can be.
When things are clean, they have very few germs.
Germs can make you sick.
So, hospitals try to keep all germs out.
They want you to get better as fast as you can.

The best part of a hospital room is the bed.
It is very comfortable.
In a hospital bed, you are high off the ground.
You can look right at your visitors when they sit in the chairs next to your bed.

If you are a patient, you may take a ride
   in a special chair.
It rolls along on wheels.
The orderly may push it for you.
The chair is called a *wheelchair*.
Only a patient can ride in it.

There are many places in the hospital to go in a wheelchair.
One place is the *X-ray department*.
The X-ray department has big cameras that take special kinds of pictures.
You will have to hold very still while the camera takes your X-ray picture.
But it doesn't hurt a bit.
X rays show the doctors the inside of your body.
An X-ray picture can show a broken bone.

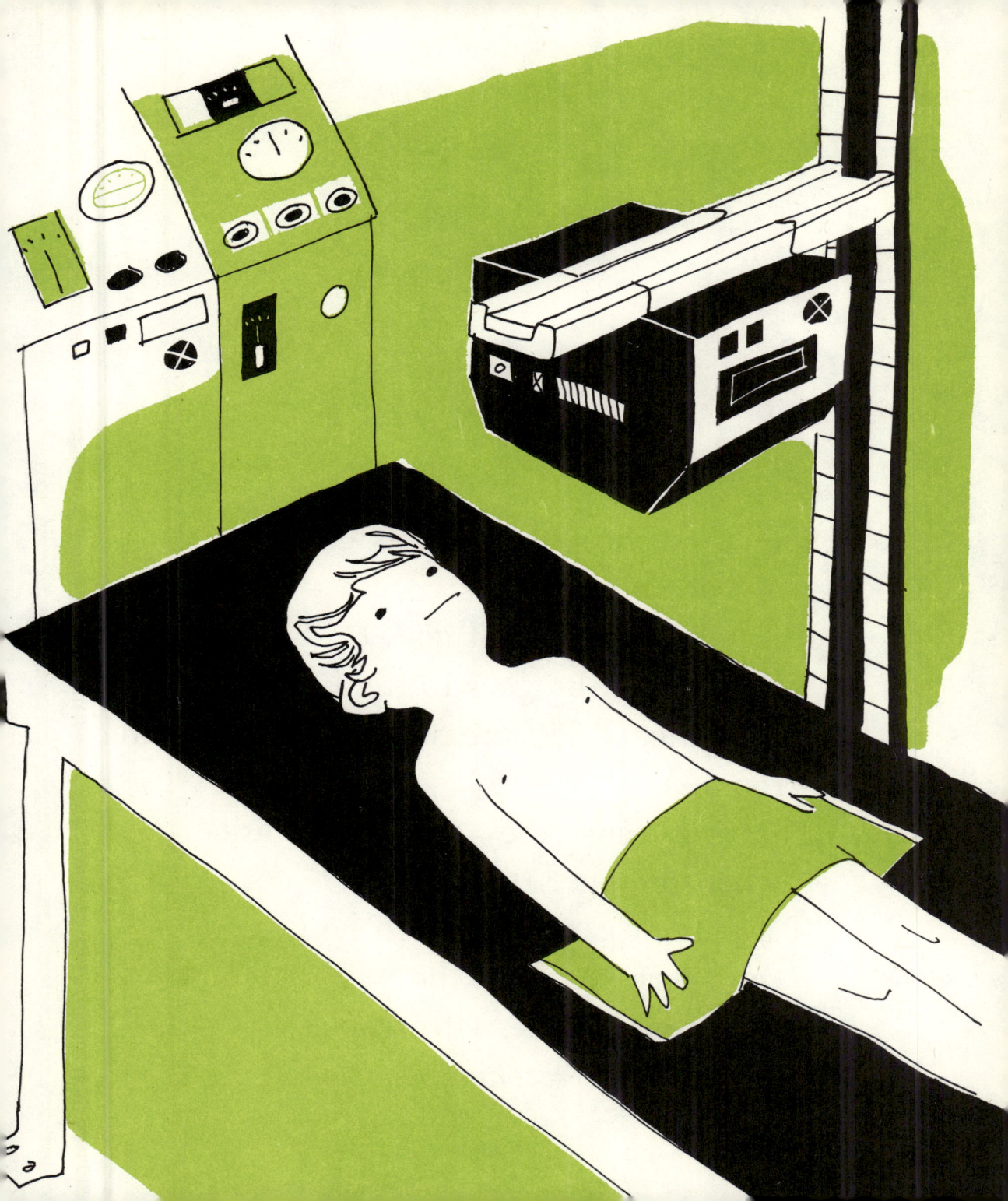

Sometimes hospital patients go to the *operating room*.
But not every patient goes to the operating room when he goes to the hospital.
Most patients don't remember the operating room.
That is because they are usually asleep when they get there.
If a patient is awake when he goes to the operating room, he will remember riding on a table with wheels.
It is called a *stretcher*.

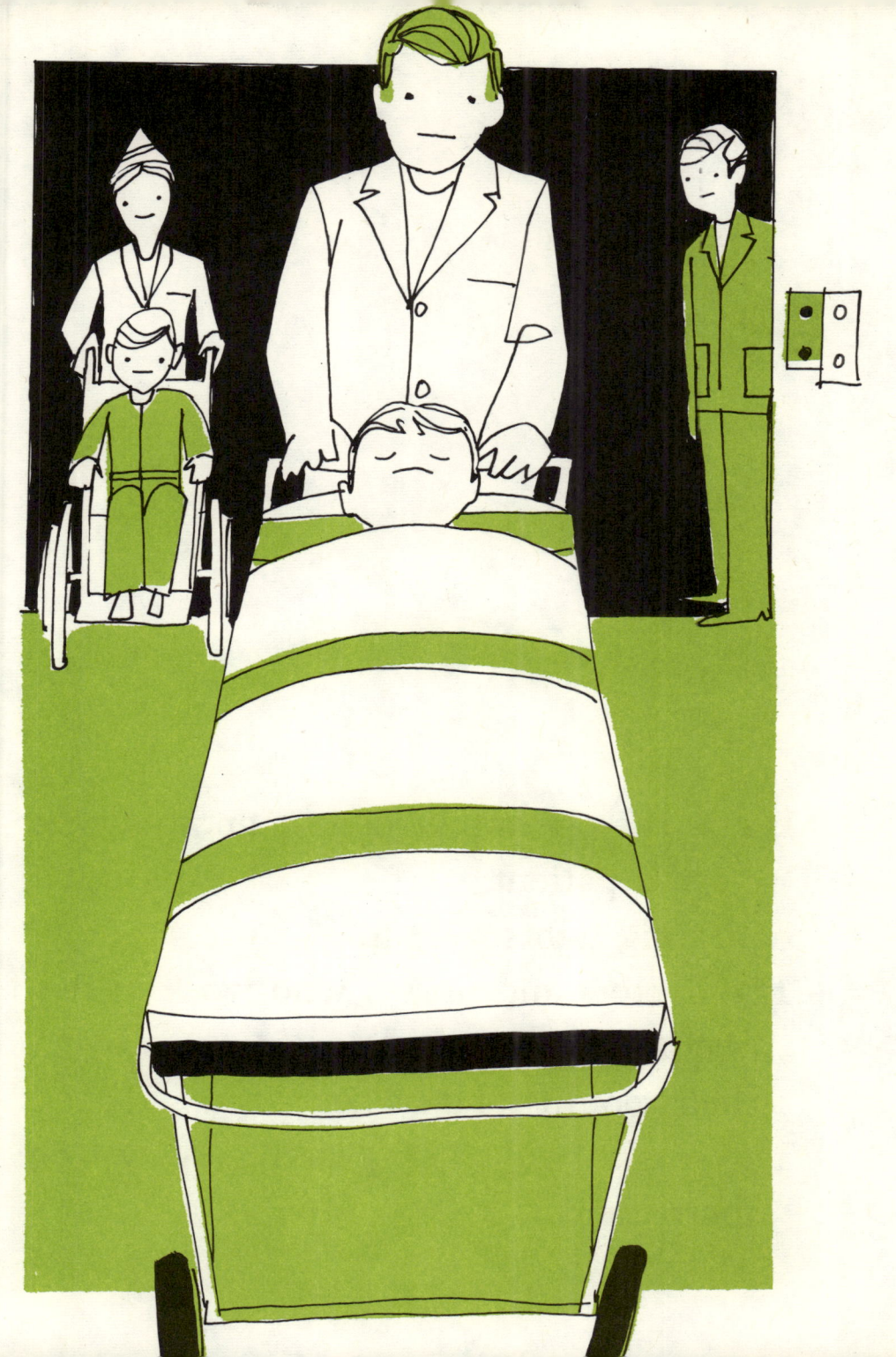

Inside the operating room is another table for the patient.
It has big lights over it.
The doctors and nurses who work in the operating room wear cloth masks over their mouths and noses.
The masks help to keep germs away from the patient.

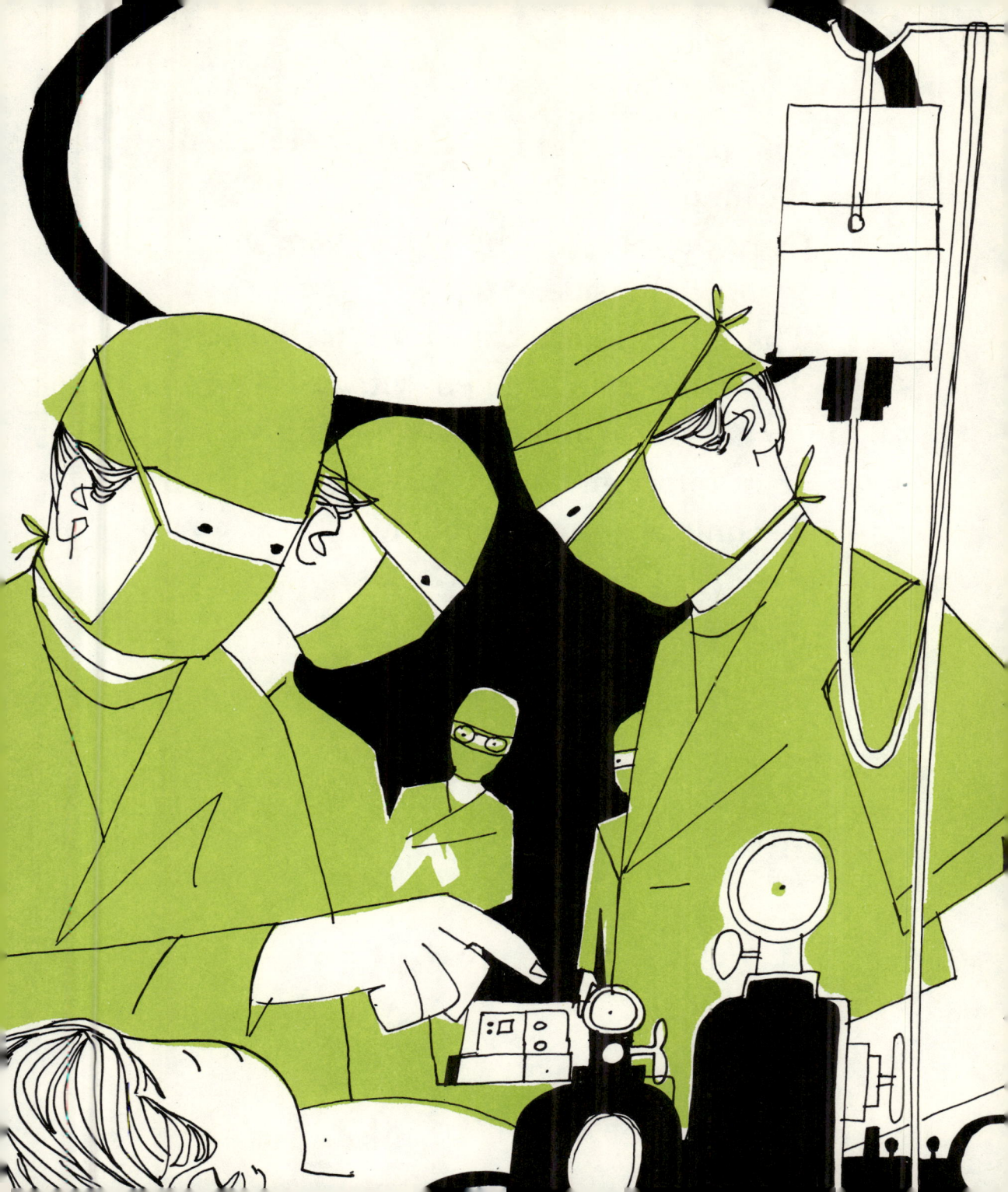

One place in the hospital that a patient cannot go is the *laboratory*.
Only the people who work there are allowed inside.
These people are called *lab technicians*.
The laboratory is filled with glass bottles and tubes and many other things.
It is a very important place.
Technicians in the laboratory look for the germs that cause sickness.

You can't go to the laboratory.
But part of it can come to you.
Sometimes a technician will bring a small
   metal basket to your room.
In the basket are glass tubes and bottles
   from the laboratory.

The technician may take a small sample of your blood.
Your doctor wants him to examine it in the laboratory.

Children who are patients have a special place to stay in the hospital.
It is called *pediatrics*.
No one but children can stay there.
Grown-ups can come to visit in pediatrics.
And doctors and nurses are allowed inside.
But only children can stay.

If you are a patient in pediatrics, you will find toys to play with.

And games.

And lots of books.

Every patient has his own bed in pediatrics.

Some beds are very tall cribs for very small children.

Some beds are regular hospital beds for bigger girls and boys.

Sometimes the rooms have pictures on the walls.
And bright curtains at the windows.
Even the tables and chairs are built just for boys and girls.
It is fun to have your own table and chair in your room.
You may even be able to watch television.

Nurses who work in pediatrics know lots
 of games.
And they can teach you new songs to sing.
They help you to get well quickly.
If you have to stay in bed, your nurse will
 fix up a special kind of table.
It fits right over your legs in the bed.
You can put a coloring book and crayons
 on it.
You can play a game on it or make a
 model airplane.

You can also use your special table for breakfast or lunch or dinner.
Your table stays right by your bed all the time.
You can even move it yourself.
It has little rolling wheels that slide around easily.

But maybe you won't have to stay in bed on pediatrics.
Then the nurse will help you to sit at the table in your room.
You can eat your meals at the table.
It's like going to a restaurant.
But this time you eat in your pajamas and slippers!

When you are a patient, your doctor may want you to take medicine.

It will help you get well quickly.

At medicine-time, the nurse will wheel a big cart into your room.

The cart holds many paper cups filled with all kinds of medicines.

Next to each cup is a card with the patient's name on it.

So, the nurse knows which medicine is just for you.

Visiting-time in the hospital is the best time of all.
The nurse will help you to get ready.
She will see that your hair is nicely combed.
She will help you to sit up in bed or sit at your table.
Then you can watch the hands of the clock moving to visiting-time.
It is good to see your family or someone else you know.

Soon it is time to get ready for bed.
The nurse will help you to brush your
 teeth and get washed.
Then she will help you into bed.
The nurse will pull up the rails around
 your bed.
The rails make sure that you don't fall out
 of the high bed when you are sleeping.

You will sleep safely in your hospital bed until the next morning.
Perhaps you will wake up feeling much, much better.
Then it may be time to go home.

DATE DUE

MAR 27 '89			
MAY 4 '90			
OCT 25 '90			
GAYLORD			PRINTED IN U.S.A.